TORN

Books by C. Dale Young

*The Second Person*  2007

*The Day Underneath the Day*  2001

# TORN

C. Dale Young

FOUR WAY BOOKS
TRIBECA

Please direct all inquiries to:
Editorial Office
Four Way Books
POB 535, Village Station
New York, NY 10014
www.fourwaybooks.com

Library of Congress Cataloging-in-Publication Data

Young, C. Dale.
  Torn / C. Dale Young.
     p. cm.
  ISBN 978-1-935536-06-2 (pbk. : alk. paper)
  I. Title.
  PS3625.O96T67 2011
  811'.6--dc22

                              2010032297

This book is manufactured in the United States of America
and printed on acid-free paper.

Four Way Books is a not-for-profit literary press. We are grateful
for the assistance we receive from individual donors, public arts agencies,
and private foundations.

This publication is made possible with public funds
from the National Endowment for the Arts

and from the New York State Council on the Arts, a state agency.

Distributed by University Press of New England
One Court Street, Lebanon, NH 03766

[clmp]

We are a proud member of the Council of Literary Magazines and Presses.

To the physicians who helped teach me the art of Medicine

&

To Donald Justice (1925-2004), who helped teach me the science of Poetry

*Denn alles Fleisch, es ist wie Gras*
*und alle Herrlichkeit des Menschen*
*wie des Grases Blumen.*
*Das Gras ist verdorret*
*und die Blume abgefallen.*


For all flesh is as grass,
and all the glory of man
as the flower of grass.
The grass withereth,
and the flower falleth away.


—from *Ein deutsches Requiem*

# Contents

## I

## II

I

# Windows

Who ever knew that light could be so blue—
not even the light traversing the windows
in Beacon Hill was ever so blue, the once

translucent glass brought from Italy
transformed by Boston weather into the sickly
blue of blue bloods. There is a story to be told.

Today, the blue water goblet is all that remains
of that history. And blue is its own story. Here,
in such blue light, I am the falling man, and you

the purpled dove, and you the six-edged star
that is brilliant but not bright. It is said
the most difficult things to paint are one's hands

or eyes. Yours have a speck of light in the right
upper quadrant of the iris and four shades of brown,
the darkest at the outermost edge; and yours,

lit up and sparkling with the reflections
of the jeweled chandelier dangling overhead.
The story isn't a difficult one to start, the way

a painter, after collecting many images,
approaches the canvas with something akin
to longing or need. How Rembrandt

understood so clearly the darkest quality
of our eyes is beyond us. But there is much
we will never understand. Darkness is its own

sad story. And mine? It begins like this:
*Listen, outside there are two great trees,*
*their branches wild, twisted, and twisting . . .*

## La Revancha del Tango

In my mouth, song. In my ear, your own song:
so much *amor*, this dance . . . The chin cocked

to facilitate a sidelong glance, the arch
of the back, the quick spark of Santa Maria

that races from thigh to knee to ball of the foot,
the stamp, that singular sound, the sound

of *you-will-have-me-tonight*. Arch
of the back, the return of your body

to mine. Spanish guitar, the slicked-back
black hair, and Santa Maria of the evening

who invites all that is forbidden in public:
the hand on shoulder, the hand on back,

on waist, the perspiration a glue
between curve of hand and the curve

of the neck. Santa Maria of Argentina, I pray
to you, to this beautiful man who follows

my lead. No flowers, no rose in my teeth.
I carry only song in my mouth.

What some call lust, others call *the calculation*.
We were fooled by the Virgin, by the music's

instructions to love. Santa Maria of Argentina,
flower behind her ear, the mouth about to sing

the song of laughter. Virgin-goddess, necessary whore—
There is, indeed, a subtle logic to seduction.

# En Fuego

The afternoon is hot. Simple, but true.
The afternoon is what, smoldering? Unlikely.
Muggy, hot, but not sweltering, not smoldering.

There is no eternal flame in this heat.
There is nothing but the unfortunate realization
of a body, my own, sweating. This is the result

of heat. Gauguin spoke of heat in the eyes
of the subject, how one should extinguish it.
Of course I would turn to someone else

to understand my own ridiculous desires.
Heat. Hot. I take my shirt off because of it.
And in your eyes I see what, a flame?

Unlikely. But there is something there,
a flickering, something that speaks
without speaking. Window to the soul

as clichéd as the heart burning with desire.
Again, heat, burning. I cannot get away from it.
Dear God, what was it You placed in the heart,

not of necessity, but because it is the center
of all moral forces and impulses? Your eyes
are flickering in this heat. What flame simmers

us this way? *En fuego*, the flame even burns
in our mother tongue, just like that.
"There is fog over the ocean," you say. "Look at it."

Don't worry, it will make its way to us eventually.
Yes. Why talk now of fire, of flames? I am shirtless
and your eyes are flickering with heat. There is a fire

in your eyes. There is a fire in my chest.
Ah yes. That is what God placed in the heart.
Let us be like flames this afternoon.

Let us smolder and consume each other, here.
In every man's heart, in the center, there is lust.
I lick it from your skin. You taste it on mine.

# Reciprocity

It almost never seemed like Paradise,
the harbor's widened grin, the loud disease
of children's cries in the surf, and green, yes green
the water's slick response to afternoon.
Not green, the travel books report, but turquoise.
But even that is insufficient praise,
this verdigrised metal melted and left behind
by a clubfooted minor Roman god.

The tourists never get it right. They start
by seeing Agamemnon striding
down the beach, while all along it's only
Argawal, the butcher's son, whose voice
in song cuts cleaner than his father's knives.
My father understands work and blood,
the labor of the men in the tired fields,
the hardened ones who hold down several jobs.

Argawal, let's call him that, brings me paper
while singing an aria from *La Bohème*, brings me
the paper he made in printing school. I offer
so little in return; I tell him stories
stolen from ancient texts he has not read.
And when the subject of verse comes up, I tell him
what my father says, that ink isn't stronger
than blood, that words can lie, the heart can too.

# The Kiss

If $E=mc^2$, then how fast is my mind moving right now?
Follow me: there is a boy in the cane fields
praying not to be found. It is not the father's belt—
no, that is only a small source of fear—but the other

boys that frighten him, the boys who beat him, kick him.
And then, as if to puzzle, the biggest of them will hold
him down, kiss him, the bully's hands unbuckling
belts. In this, children are no different.

Anything else in the world seems better
than this image, these boys. Schoolyard, noontime,
the clearing just beyond the wide expanse of cane,
the shallow caves down by the seaside.

Follow me: can words really hurt? Do actions
speak louder? *Sissy, homo, faggot.* Could these
be real ammunition? There is a beach in Ibiza,
not a cane field in sight. There, in the early evening,

I saw a man bend slowly to kiss another man.
I assumed they were lovers. I assumed they
had known each other for many years
or had met at a bar earlier that afternoon.

The young Italian who had been kissed rose
and walked along the shore toward me. As he passed,
I told him it was beautiful, that kiss. But the mind
is never fast enough, you see. It is never fast enough.

The eyes saw what they wanted to see, saw tenderness.
But there was nothing like that there. The kiss?
It had been a warning. The kiss meant *change your ways
or risk harm*. Brutish, that tenderness. Sharp, too.

# Blood

Someone has already pulled a knife
across my chest, and the rope has already
gripped our wrists drawing blood.

I am naked, and I cannot be sure
if you are as well. In the room, the men
come and go, yelling *blood bath*, *half-blood*,

*blood-bitch*. We never hear the word *trueblood*.
In my dreams I am dying all the time.
We are bound and gagged, blindfolded,

but still I know you must be the one
lying there, the cool anodized steel table
beneath us, the two of us side by side.

Lying there, my shoulder blades ache,
and there is blood collecting in
the corners of my mouth. But then it happens,

just as it always happens: your fingers
suddenly twist into tiny shoots, your arms
break free as you accept the shape

of a tree, the leaves sprouting, the delicate
bark rising up from your skin's surface.
Try as I might, I never seem able.

On the telephone this morning, I again
keep the dream to myself. Half-blood
becomes half-breed. Blood-bitch

becomes blood-sister. But blood never lies,
does it? Blood carries so many secrets
one can only hear its murmurs in our arteries,

its incessant monologue, in the quiet
night's bed just before sleep. Blood says
*You are more* and, sometimes, *You are less.*

# Fourteen

Bless me Father, for I have sinned. It has been
six days since my last confession. I let a guy
cheat off of my science test because it made me
feel smarter. And I ignored my mother telling me

to be home by 9:00 pm. I don't really even know
why she asks such things. And I continue to have
impure thoughts, sometimes every hour. I let a
girl kiss me, a boy, too, but we all had our clothes on.

And this may not be a sin, but I knocked Mike down
on the basketball court just as he was making a jump,
just to be able to help him up, help him back
to the locker room. His knee got twisted. It swelled

until it looked like a softball. It was so swollen.
He let me hold ice to it until his folks came.
I liked holding the ice to it. But I found myself
having impure thoughts, Father, strange thoughts.

I sat there holding the ice and staring at his knee
and up the legs of his shorts. I could see
the white edge of his jockey shorts and more.
I had to look, Father. I had to look.

Forgive me, I couldn't help it, the staring.
It was like the time last week, after the game,
when I couldn't help but watch the soap suds
under your chin just before you washed off.

I sat on a bench in my towel and watched you, the
shape of your back, your arms, your chest. I know
this is wrong, Father, watching you in the shower.
But I only watched the soap. I only watched the water.

# Clean

Already his abdomen was sculpted, and already
the thin trail descending from beneath his belly button.
Even now it is difficult to explain it. I was, after all,
only 7; I didn't even know what Turkish meant.

In the dead of winter, which only meant
certain flowers had ceased blooming on the island,
we had driven up into the mountains
to "take the waters," as our parents put it.

Our parents' instructions were simple: they would be
in one room, our sisters in another, my brother
and I in yet another. Down the dark hallways
as dark as tunnels, down through the strong smell

of minerals and seawater, the attendants led us
to our rooms. What was that smell? Sulfur?
Aluminum? There was the smell of salt, but it
was not the salt of the earth, not the sea itself.

The old man told us not to sit in the water for more
than fifteen minutes at a time, to drink lots of cold water,
to scrub the salts into our skin, to take care of each other.
And then, he left us. We took off our clothes, did it

without thinking. "You get in first," is all he said, his voice
sounding more like my father's, his voice having changed
almost a year ago. His body had changed, too.
Sitting in the pool, my thoughts began to swim

in the vapors, the steam. I felt nauseated.
I wanted not to look at him. I wanted to look at the tile:
blue and blue-white with the depiction of a terrible vine
twisting and creeping around the tops of the walls.

When he got out and lay on the tile next to the pool,
his abdomen was already sculpted, and the thin trail . . .
He knew I watched him, and he loved the admiration.
When I finally got out, my head dizzy, my heart racing

from the heat, I lay myself down next to him. He scrubbed
my back with a rough sponge, pulled me against his chest
as he scrubbed behind my ears and under my arms. There,
in the steam, I was cleaner than I would ever be again.

# Body & Soul

I

The Devil lives in that field.
              I have seen him a hundred times.

The rust-colored creek,
           the dead and dying trees
                               that ring the dying
grass . . .

I have seen the Devil
                creeping

          through that field at night, flickering

like moonlight through the leaves of trees.

I tell you the boy deserved it,
                    that fool running
       through that field in the storm.

No reason
            to be out in that storm. No animals
        to be brought back in. And the Devil
                  struck him. The Devil

struck him, but he lives. He is marked.

II

What was my excuse with you?
You were the right sex, and the right height.
Even the speed of the trees as we raced
the road to Blue Springs was right.

But the springs, blue like their name,
betrayed the future as I stood there lying
that there would be someone else, someone
who would take me away from you.

But sometimes lies become the truth.
Sometimes the soul speaks out without prompting.
While you reveled in the oddity of green autumn
in Florida, I was leaving, was already gone.

III


Everything we do
                    requires charge, small
           electrical impulses
racing through our bodies.

          In many ways
we are all conductors.
                  In Bed 9, the living
proof. A man, age 29, struck
                    by lightning in a field.

I have no need for him
               to remove his shirt, but I ask him
     to take it off
so I can better listen to his lungs.

His back is like a drawing at Lascaux,
                 blood
marking his skin
             instead of red clay—

a branching tree, the form lightning took
          as it traveled through him.

I ask him if it hurts.

He tells me
he hasn't seen it, but friends
have told him it is

like the lone oak
standing in the field behind his house.

IV


And then, the one I believed to be my soulmate.
Outside, in the stagnant air of coastal Virginia,
I wondered how I had been caught, laid to rest
with such a man. At Water's Edge, a street

nowhere near water's edge, I watched the dead leaves
flitter across the parking lot. Somewhere, a bottle was
being opened, and the soul was being poured
for us into crystal goblets, the soul red

and full-bodied, its nose hinting of berries
and bright earth waiting to be consumed.
Who could resist the taste of it?
Piece by piece, it took you. It almost took me.

V

Everything dies out there.

I remember
                    how they strung people up
in that field.

              Thieves, prostitutes, murderers—
they hung them in that field.
                              Blood brings

the Devil. Things die there. Things are called there
       to die.
                    I have warned him
                              a hundred times,
and he lives because the Devil is in him,

stupid boy whose very father died in that field.

They say blood is thicker than water.
                    Not this time. The Devil
       is in him, sure as thunder.

He is marked. And in that tree, there is a serpent.

## VI

In the city at the very edge of the Pacific,
I stood in the rain for hours for the one I love.
There was no body left, the clothes and flesh
having run off in search of a drain.

All left was the soul and its attendant concerns.
When the sun appeared in late afternoon,
when my feet ached and *understood* the day's longevity,
there was nothing but wisps of cloud hanging on.

Who doesn't want to believe one is made
for someone else? This morning, a deer darted away
as I descended into the canyon. It was a sign, I'm sure,
like the blue springs, like the red soul lying in a glass.

# The Bridge

I love. Wouldn't we all like to start
a poem with "I love . . ."? I would.
I mean, I love the fact there are parallel lines
in the word "parallel," love how

words sometimes mirror what they mean.
I love mirrors and that stupid tale
about Narcissus. I suppose
there is some Narcissism in that.

You know, Narcissism, what you
remind me to avoid almost all the time.
Yeah, I love Narcissism. I do.
But what I really love is ice cream.

Remember how I told you
no amount of ice cream can survive
a week in my freezer. You didn't believe me,
did you? No, you didn't. But you know now

how true that is. I love
that you know my Achilles heel
is none other than ice cream—
so chilly, so common.

And I love fountain pens. I mean
I just love them. Cleaning them,
filling them with ink, fills me
with a kind of joy, even if joy

is so 1950. I know, no one talks about
joy anymore. It is even more taboo
than love. And so, of course, I love joy.
I love the way joy sounds as it exits

your mouth. You know, the *word* joy.
How joyous is that. It makes me think
of bubbles, chandeliers, dandelions.
I love the way the mind runs

that pathway from bubbles to dandelions.
Yes, I love a lot. And right here,
walking down this street,
I love the way we make

a bridge, a suspension bridge
—almost as beautiful as the
Golden Gate Bridge—swaying
as we walk hand in hand.

# The Second Omen: Spring

One refuses to hold the other's hand.
One pours wine and misses the glass.
Signs sent by a lesser god again and again
to no avail. That the body is mostly water,

this we could agree upon. All else was less
than palatable. I said I loved you, too.
In this way, the heart lies, too.
The dogwoods bloom; their lies, like mine,

gorgeous and capable of seduction.
And outside, the vines kept twisting and twisting . . .
Yes, outside, the vines kept twisting and twisting,
gorgeous and capable of seduction.

The dogwood's blooms are lies like mine.
In this way, the heart lies, too.
Palatable? I said I loved you, too.
This we could agree upon. All else was less,

to no avail. The body is still mostly water.
Signs. Lesser gods. Again and again,
one pours wine and misses the glass,
one refuses to hold the other's hand.

II

# Few Shall Answer

*Many are called*
*to burn at least one thing they once owned . . .*
—Rick Barot

You write that many are called, but Etruscan
murals are what come to mind, a neighbor's
coffee-table book filled with blank pages below

a lithograph, its image stolen from a decrepit church.
Where are the many, my friend? In a factory,
or on a farm struggling in the dark before the rooster?

Are they out trimming the hedges while the mist
lifts from the countryside, entire walls
of it evaporating into the stagnant air?

Sometimes the sea shimmers in its oily
skin, the cliff sides climb into a clean
light, and everything—almost everything—is

as it should be. But for now, the girl
lying bent double on the railing is a Piero
painting coming apart, her shirt unbuttoning,

the leaflets of her hem, her dress
billowing like bad weather.
Many are called. Many are called into

their madness, the voices along the cliffs moving in
and out of their ears as they did before,
as they did when no one

yet knew the word *schizophrenia*.
What great multitude, what great assembly
is called to mind? Many are called into the air,

right here along the Pacific's edge, and are
taken up in a draft and buoyed. Seeing things in
this way, how could I not believe there was another way,

that the body taken from the bridge was merely opening
at its seams, its bad humors spilling. But nothing
can reverse the terror and the heart quickening

as the body then falls away from you. Was my own heart
incapable of recognizing dread in that woman's final moment?
I once heard a woman explain that her stillborn

son had cried against her chest, his breath
furrowing under button after button
of her hospital gown, his breath terribly

quick in the way it shifted and fingered
her skin. Is this how the mind stops?
Many are called to do so many things, my friend.

And, as always, few shall answer.

# Inheritance

*Long Dead.* He had been *Long Dead.* Such an odd phrase.
How long is *Long Dead*? How many moons is that?
But my use of the words "many moons" offended
my great-uncle, who raised his eyebrows and mumbled
that I should stop speaking like a pansy. I did not
know then that flowers could speak. I wasn't old enough.
I rehearsed the words in my head, repeating them
with various inflections: many moons, many moons.
And when I tired, I shouted that there was a murder
of crows in the yard. Ah the English sneer, the slight curl
of the upper lip and the flaring of the tight nostrils.
Great Uncle barked something about a gaggle of geese.
When it was pointed out there were no crows in the yard,
oh the looks, the shaking of heads, the word liar
and, again, pansy. Yes, I was alive by the Grace of God.
By the Grace of God: it sounded so lovely, so pristine.
Grace, that beautiful but difficult thing to divine,
and God, well, God was God. The teacup returned
to its saucer so quickly it broke. The book glided,
like the quickest of jaybirds, into the kitchen window.
What had I said? What could I possibly have said?
That William Richard Extant August would have killed me,
that he should have killed my mother, is all I remember
my great-uncle shouting. I was not a real man, a man's
man, a man of guts, a pure man, an honorable man.
In the portrait of him near the sunroom, his head tilted
between direct stare and a sly, almost feminine, profile,
there was a mole on the upper inner edge of his left earlobe.
William Richard Extant August, I had never met you.

I had never killed anything with my bare hands.
And years later, having learned to shave, I find it.
There, on my ear, the same mole, in the same spot.
*Long Dead*? No, not dead at all. Asleep. Resting.
Waiting for the right time to make himself known.

# Nature

Half-joking, half-serious, seriously halved,
I wanted to find Him in the empty sleeve
of air surrounding the bell's clapper.

Would He not be found there, hovering
in the air prepared to carry sound? So many
silly ideas the adolescent carries around.

So many of us vowed chastity, the easy gesture
for those who had denied their own nature.
But Nature could not be ignored—the way it

snaps the heads off mice, takes the hatchlings
one by one, breaks the mule's back. I understood
the rules. We all did. Rule #1: show kindness

to your brother. I wanted to show more
than kindness, wanted to favor my brothers,
for lack of a better word. Rule #2: do unto others . . .

I won't even go there. What point in that now?
There was always God reclining in the empty space
beside my hand, beside the thenar eminence,

beside my careful eyes that imagined the other
boys in all of their happiness. In every man, God
had placed Himself. In every man, I sought

to touch that God. Silly, I know. Silly.
What I wanted then was to break God's heart—
I wanted Him to snap my neck, break my back.

# Paying Attention

*I know everything about my God.*
*Can you tell me about your own?*

Outside the window, rain. Well, the sound
of rain. Why would I start this way?
Because my God prefers a preamble—
Spool of lightning, Fist of night-blooming jasmine.

My God can slice me clean open from head
to the arches of my feet, does so easily
with a swipe of His index fingernail, a clean
slice to show you the back half of me

seen from the front. He sometimes puts me
back together again. But with my front half
gone, He licks the back wall of my throat,
His tongue like sweetened gasoline.

The sound of rain against my window
is louder than expected, is my God
reminding me to pay attention. And my God
despises inattention and punishes me often

for it. He strips me of my clothes and lashes
my back with his cat-o-nine-tails. I am
quick to cry, so quick to promise humility. I am
a liar. I am weak and a liar. And I am punished.

What more can I tell you? What can I say
to explain my God? He has little tolerance
for hatred. He expects undying love
and affection. He leaves the large red

imprints of his fist against my back,
sometimes flowering on my face. He showers
me with expectations. He lifts me up
to remind me of my foolish fear of heights.

# Recitativo

As an arrow flies through the air, some
will say it swims because it bends and flexes
from side to side, like a fish does, like a fish swims.
But is that true? True, but not exact.
It isn't enough to say the arrow swims.
It isn't enough to say the arrow quivers.

Remember the spine of the arrow is wood.
It cannot be aluminum because such things
were not yet known in that world—the spine
limber enough to avoid the drawn bow's shattering.
Know that the arrow does not serve the bow.
Know that the bow does not serve the arrow.

Not powder blue, but powdery and blue.
Not bound to a tree, but hands strung up to a tree.
Distinctions like these are, in fact, important
when the time comes for you to recount the story.
It isn't enough to say the arrows flew.
It isn't enough to say the arrows pierced.

The turkey doesn't fly nor does it swim.
But its feathers are essential for the arrow
to meet its target. The air is a swarm of arrows
and, for less than a minute, it could be called beautiful.
Know that the arrow, now arrows, will strike the flesh.
Know that the arrows, now arrow, will meet the target.

This is an old story, powdery lens of time having made
the light of it softer, almost as sweet as this music.
You must tell it. You will tell it. The man's head refuses
to slump. It cocks to one side, the eyes refusing to shut.
It isn't enough to say they killed the man.
It is never enough to say he became a saint.

# Quiet City

Dearest Heart, the leaves have stopped
fluttering away from the trees, and the sky
steadies itself above a city

circled only by pigeons this evening.
The street is absent its cars and their horns,
silence placed on us now like a dream.

Even the clicking sound of the keys
under my anxious fingers is missing.
Instead, I pull a stylus across this page,

let the ink slip from the nib without a sound.
I have resurrected the old fountain pen
but not the zeal of the wide-eyed young poet

anxious to record each and every thing
seen from the window's vantage.
What I watch this evening are pigeons,

their greys like the clouds that drifted over
the river this morning carrying scraps of paper,
bits and pieces of reports and memos

that minute after minute lightly dusted us
as we stood in the street watching the sky.
The river continues slipping by, my love,

and night slowly throws its spell across the yards
erasing all of those white and yellow scraps
covered with words and words and more words—

I may never find the right words to describe this.

# Stone and Fire

The sea sounds its regrets against rocks each year.
None of us had learned a kind of gentleness,
and this one could hear in our words, sharp as they were

as they sank through the air on our porches. Fire
is what comes to mind when I think of us talking, the sea
and its endless murmur nothing but backdrop like trees.

How odd that the mind would settle on heat and fire
to describe the words that fell among us, not gold
or the golden, but the raw flicker that consumes things

indiscriminately. What privilege affords such liars?
To speak of Life, we mentioned paintings by Renoir
and the flawless sonnet that recounted the wall

that circled Eden. But the time for such talk is gone.
Sometimes, perhaps, it is easier to forget than to recall
how men each day die with visions offered by fools

like us. Stone and Fire, Fire and Stone—
we kill as we always have. And we choose not to believe.
We continue living; we refuse to grieve.

# At Camp Galileo

Newton's rotten heart has yet to fall from the tree,
and the Earth has just begun to orbit the sun,
the sun just becoming the center of the universe.
The children are reclining on benches with
their laptop computers, and God is still

a mystery. How like God to be still, a mystery.
The orbit of moons, heft and heresy:
all seems explainable here. And the children
seem intent on learning the fine art
of subterfuge, of silence and the ability to plot.

It is lunchtime or the time just after lunchtime.
It will be a good two hours before
the parents begin arriving. The children here
believe they can chart the course of God in the sky
better than they can the motion of the spheres.

And Einstein, well, Einstein is a shadow
under the great oak tree, just a shadow.
Out on Brotherhood Way, the traffic moves
with the regularity of comets, with the regularity
of counselors who circumnavigate to spy on each

of the pupils. Their shadows are small in this light,
their shadows close-cropped and close to the body.
What motion there is appears suspended
here in the eyes of God and Man. And then,
the young girl yelling *Eureka!* She has found

the right entry on Wikipedia. The counselors
are happy. The other children are happy.
Everyone suddenly seems buoyant and happy.
Above the yellowed, dying grass, a jovial ignorance.
It is not much different than my own ignorance.

# The Seventh Circle

The Church warns there is no heaven
for us—that our behavior can only bring hell,
an absence of dawn, an endless twilight
in which we will never feel the strong hands
we are used to—that we will be forgotten,
our names left purposely in the shadows.

We claim to enjoy the shadows
of this world, the nights, the heaven
of a lover's body never wholly forgotten,
that to forget the body is our only hell.
Look carefully. Look at these hands
veined by this stained-glass twilight

that only differs from twilight
in its excess color, in its lack of shadows.
Look at Veronica, the way she hands
her veil to the Christ and secures her heaven.
Look at Judas dancing in the flames of hell,
the pieces of silver left forgotten

in a weedy field now forgotten
by everything except twilight.
Did Michelangelo dream of hell
while he manipulated shadows
in an attempt to show us heaven?
Did he betray himself with his hands

that admired the strength of other men's hands?
If he did, we have forgotten.
Yes. Here we see the luxuries of heaven,
the bodies clothed only in light
languishing above painted shadows
that separate these glories from hell.

There will be no Cerberus in our circle of hell,
we are told, only hundreds of swaying hands
reaching up from even darker shadows.
If we have sinned, we have forgotten.
Outside the church, I try to forget the twilight,
forget the 5,040 prerequisites for heaven.

# In the Chen Style

·

The body remembers the Form, by which
I mean *my* body remembers the Form.

·

Within a stand of pines, I sink like a stone.

·

The arms, my arms, recall the slicing motion
of hand and upturned palm. I am here
to stand my ground. I am here, pretending
to remember.

·

And blood keeps repeating its songs
in my ears. Same songs, over and over.
Blood runs roughshod in my chest.

·

My arms remember. Even my legs remember.

◆

Slow is the stone sinking at the edge of the field.
Slow, the old books falling from the shelves and
the light drawing dust through the air.

◆

And the body sounds a lot like Sting today, sings:
*A lesson once learned, so hard to forget.*

◆

But I am dim, darling, and I
cannot remember a thing.

◆

I run through the yard yelling:
Brother tree. Brother hawk. Brother grass!
I do this because it is so unlike me.

◆

And the words I cannot remember?
Oh, I find them.

•

With each movement of the Form, they come back:
*Cloud hands; The World; Wind in trees; Flower in its bed.*


•


I call a piece of toast, Sally. I name the statue
on the terrace, Becky. Words, just words.
I am here to forget each and every thing you taught me.

# Or Something Like That

In the yard today, the pine needles began snowing
down. The way they caught the light was curious.
And the maple's leaves, all red and ochre, were

already littering the walkway. I, well I sat
thinking the same dark thoughts I have had
since childhood. You know the ones. I need

not explain them to You, of all people.
But it is so easy to call things dark thoughts,
a kind of lazy shorthand. Too easy to forget

the maxim that everyone is good in Your eyes.
We both know this is not true, is a lie. I mean,
the high school counselor they put away for life...

How can he be good in Your eyes? Sometimes,
I am convinced no one is good in Your eyes.
Dark thoughts, yes. I am doubting again.

I doubt the pine needles, the maple leaves,
the robin carrying on its stupid song,
my own voice mumbling on a slate blue terrace.

Easy to doubt. Always easy. And the old Jesuit
who lectured me on this? Well, he doubted, too.
But I am not quite ready to be broken just yet.

I have a few things left in me, a few surprises.
No magic is as good as Your magic, but I have
hidden cards up my sleeve, twisted the handkerchief,

slipped the coin behind my watch. I still have
a few tricks left to play. And the light shifting
on the terrace, the pine needles coming down,

I know what they mean. I get what You are trying
to get at. I am here, God, I am here. I am waiting
for You to blind me with a sunstorm of stars.

# The Moss Garden

Somewhere outside Kyoto's line, she said,
they stumbled across the famous garden of moss,
the smallish sign so plain it could have been
overlooked. No temple, only moss.
So they entered the walkway with little expectation,
the silence creeping in, much like expectation.

Instead of leading them to the garden directly,
two monks had led them to a different task,
requested they copy three hundred characters,
the ink and paper set down for the task.
And this, too, was a practiced form of prayer,
left behind for those who had forgotten prayer.

The monks left brushes, ink, and bowls of water.
They asked the seekers to write, to pray. But prayer,
any prayer, wasn't easy. The brush and ink,
the doubting hand, made not for simple prayer.
And even as I write this, I do not want to pray.
This story changes nothing; I do not want to pray.

# Late Poem

*In memoriam Donald Justice (1925-2004)*

The late evening fog comes quickly in again,
pours over the same San Francisco you once loved.
Now, the silence is what I notice most
here along the Great Highway, the flowers
brighter now for lack of simple sunlight.
You didn't die in the rain. You didn't die
in Miami. And I cannot know, will never know,
if there was, in fact, sunlight leafing through
the papers in your room, sunlight sifting through
the half-empty trash can sitting near the bed.
Out on the Great Highway, the cars keep
moving. As you said, everything keeps moving.
But what keeps a voice moving, old friend?
What prompts us to open our mouths and sing,
once again, the same sad song you knew so well?
Orpheus could not help but turn back, his voice
falling into the black river, his eyes fixated
on the darkness within the rotting trees lining
that terrible road. So turn back, old teacher,
sing for us again with a voice now young, agile.
My song is too simple, divided both by blood
and profession. The right words? Where would I
find them? The clock laments, perhaps, what I have done
and what I have yet to do. I haven't changed much,
you know. Now, like then, my nagging indecision
translates into a late poem. Accept this one, teacher,
accept this song I can barely hum over the wind,
my voice cracking and simple, drowned out by the wind.

# Wind

But I was afraid then. I remember still
the way my feet skittered up the bamboo,
the way the air held me as the stalks bent
one way and then the other. I remember
the first steps across the tops of trees,
and then the all-consuming speed.

Unlike you, I was lit by anger then,
the least of all warriors. You were there
when the old man first found me, taught me
how to become water. And so much has passed.
River, air, everything passes. They say
the first time you give yourself up to the wind,

there shall be no fear. But I was afraid.
Yesterday, I watched one of my students
scale the bamboo for the first time.
His hands shook only when he returned
to the ground. Now, he wants to know
how to change the wind, this boy

who has only just learned to be carried by it.
Do not laugh. I remember you in the field
so long ago, your fear, your stillness,
the supreme weapon. And I remember you
stripped of your clothes washing the blood
from your feet—you, who keep my heart

in your rooms. Now, the old man says
I cannot move forward until I learn to forget,
that to become wind is to forget even this body.
I have been water propelled across the fields
from the edge of the riverbank. I have been fire
licking back the scrub outside the sad-faced grove.

But this, this final step . . . Do not laugh.
Mornings, after you study the indentation
I have left beside you on the mat, when you
walk the bamboo line between field and grove,
do not be angry with me for leaving. Look up.
The wind in the trees betrays more than the wind.

# The Argument

There is an inky darkness in certain old paintings
used, for lack of better technique, to add depth.
Of course I would notice it. Of course, you would
notice that I notice it. It wouldn't be the first time.

It is a fault. I am certain of that. But I can only hope
that recognition is the first step toward correcting this.
One could whine here and state, for the record,
how difficult it is to see the gold light clinging

to things when one lives a life attending to darker
things. But you, my friend, will not let me whine,
will not accept such a facile response from me.
So, let us agree to disagree about my faults.

There is a moment in the early morning when
the sun is not yet visible but the light is visible,
a tint of it, perhaps, advancing down the hillside.
It is my frightened hour before I don the white

lab coat, before I enter the halls of the hospital.
Always there is relish and dread at the same time.
How can I explain this to you who believe I am
incapable of tenderness in my art? I could lie

but I won't. I see darkness in the timbre
of your voice, even when you are excited,
even as your face lights up with the story of
serendipity, of how Whitman's *Leaves of Grass*

found its publisher. The shadow? I cannot help
but trust it more than the object itself. One sees
what one is meant to see. And darkness is,
I fear, an older friend. Let us leave it at that.

In the frightened hour before I don the white lab coat,
anything is possible, anything. I could return upstairs
and refuse to get dressed. I could refuse to check
with the answering service. And that, my friend

would be darkness. Tenderness? How do you
define that? I define it this way: the care to address
another's concerns with the same exacting care one expects
for himself. And this is dark. It has always been dark.

# In the Cutting Room

That the falling glass, the one
that falls 4 feet before shattering
into 18 pieces, is caught in something
between 64 and an infinite number of frames
between edge of table and the kitchen's

fake Italian marble floor . . . . This is exactly
the kind of crap I cannot stand to hear.
God in the details. God in the minutiae
of a falling body, a mass falling
through space and time. What shutter-fly genius,

what poet of a scientist discovered this?
I reject the scientific. I have
halted the glass exactly 4 inches
above the ground and reveled in the
"potential" of it. I have halted your heart

exactly 4 inches above the ground. See
how easily I revise our history? See how I
have swapped my heart for your own?
The falling heart about to shatter, held
in space, in time, by the mind's quicker-than-thou

apertures? Exactly the kind of crap I cannot stand.
I have held a heart in my own hands, the heavy
rubbery mass of it slick with blood and saline.
With forceps and dissecting probe, I have
opened each valve, studied its small ears

that sometimes fill with blood. Circumflex,
Left Anterior Descending, I have followed
the pathways blood takes around the heart.
I am not qualified to speak about God and Physick.
I have no gift for the 35-mm world of

quick shutter and quicker thought. Who does?
I speak what I know. I speak with a filthy mouth.
And what do I know? What could I possibly know?
That the heart is tougher than you think. That it
does not break. That it, too, becomes dust.

III

# The Ether Dome

How many years have passed since the first time
I stood here with the sound of traffic on Storrow
echoing like the wind in an alley? The Charles

creeps by now as it did then, slips slowly by
the almost leafless trees and the medical center
blooming at its edge. And so, the waking dream

begins again. Picture me, the quiet orderly,
observing everything in the Emergency Department:
the doctors snaking a tube down someone's throat

in search of glass, the blood and the bloodless things
we never forget. On that rare afternoon, the E.D. quiet,
no one aware of what I am supposed to be doing,

I stole away to explore the oldest parts of the hospital.
When I found the old lecture hall, the late afternoon light
collected in its center like heat, collected above

the wooden table on which techniques of surgery
had been demonstrated. I was not yet a physician, not even
a medical student. I had yet to learn the names

of each and every muscle in the body. What I knew then
was that the statue in the corner, the greying marble figure,
was Hippocrates. The other one, Apollo wearing the laurel.

So much silence in the silence of that room. So much left
unspoken there where the cries of patients had been hushed,
eventually, with the rag dipped in ether. Would I be able

to study Medicine, to open up another person's body?
When I left that room, I already knew the answer.
But there, in that dusty light, I was not yet a man.

I stood there more hopeful than I would ever be again.
Soon, I would learn the numerous ways to learn.
And soon, very soon, I would learn how to fail.

# Corpus Medicum

In the dream of fever, in the murky light
of a mind ill-at-ease, it is the tile I remember,
the single row of beige tile that circumnavigated

the laboratory, a tile that seemed more in keeping
with a bathroom decorated in the 1970s
than with a room in which to dissect cadavers.

Below the tile, a lime-like pale green, and above,
the clean white of hospitals. In the dream of fever,
I am there again in the first days trying to speak

the dead language of naming: *latissimus, pectoralis,
orbicularis oris.* For some of us, this was a language
we had heard before we could comprehend

the alpha and omega of *muscularis.* Someone
whispered that the very act of naming was holy.
*Cingularum* that became *cingulare,* the cincture

that held the cassock in place. But fever
brings much more than the simple images
of the past, brings with it the smell of the sacristy

and His Reverence standing still
as one of us undid the cincture at his waist.
O black cassock, weren't we the lucky ones,

the special boys who were allowed into the secret
rooms of the Church? In the anatomy laboratory,
my head lowered and intent on study, the smell

was anything but human—the smell of formalin
and bleach disguised the glistening corpus,
disguised the human stench. And had I not seen this

attempt at deception before, seen it as a child
when our dirty hands and mouths were covered,
all hushed by the language of Rome and perfumed

by the incense left clinging to Monsignor's large hands?
Out of one dead language another one rose easily.
*Cingularum* that became *cingulare,* cincture that became a cinch.

# Imprimatur

The ones who paint the word *Latino* on my forehead
think me lazy and careless. The ones who pin
*Asian-American* to my chest consider me a hard worker.

Unfortunately, the pulmonologist charged with
inspiring us with the tradition of the physical exam
felt I belonged to the former. You hear people

sometimes ask for a definition of cruelty
because you know they have never tried imagining
a life other than their own. And the definitions,

every last one, are pointless. Cruelty, of which we
are all capable. *See one, do one, teach one,*
we were told repeatedly. And after having seen

my teacher place a central line twice, he demanded
I jump in and place the line this woman needs.
Her veins had collapsed. I watched her watch

my hands shaking. And I could see that she saw
something like terror in my face. I am focusing
so hard on the skin near the clavicle that I can

almost count the pores there. The bore in my hand.
The pressure to break the skin greater than I thought.
And when I miss the vessel, when the needle slips

into a different space, air suddenly starts spewing
back at me from the needle's slim body, the air
a tiny whistling sound. And I see the muscles

in her neck starting to flex more, trying
to compensate for the sudden diminishment of oxygen
as her right lung collapses. I am too scared to cry.

And the pulmonologist is mumbling something
about how I now get to learn a different procedure.
He is saying something about placing a chest tube,

about re-expanding her dropped lung.
But I am not paying attention, cannot pay attention,
the woman's face, her eyes, the calmness

with which she looks at me and says that it
will be okay, that she will be fine. And when
my teacher punctures the skin and muscles between

her ribs, when the blood begins to trickle slowly
across her side, I freeze. I cannot get myself
to shove the tube into the newly made hole.

And I am lazy. I am a lazy spic, my teacher says,
his anger visible in the quickness with which he places
the tube in her chest. And when the tears start

clouding my eyes, he tells me to keep my mouth shut,
that this procedure is straightforward, is black
or white. I can barely breathe. Surely my own lungs

are collapsing. And there is anger in his voice.
The world of Medicine is black or white, he says.
And I am worried. And all I can think about

is the cru in cruelty, that cross, that crux,
and the black or white world of Medicine,
a world in which I do not even exist.

# The Personal

Wear the wedding ring on a chain around your neck.
The personal, as in personal life? Say nothing.
This is how I spoke to myself then. These are the things

I used to remind myself daily. Gender neutral.
Only use gender neutral when you must talk
about your beloved. And never speak of love.

It will only invite questions. So much to learn.
Memorize all of it. Know it well enough to recite
it backwards if you must. Every last detail.

The expected heart rate of a newborn? The exact
percentage of fats, protein, and carbohydrates
in Total Parenteral Nutrition? The formulae

for calculating blood volume? Everything.
You have no time for the personal.
And that morning, on my last day in the NICU?

Do I remember it? I do. I still remember it.
And this is what I say to myself now: You must
remember it. Along with the calculations, the hours

and hours of sick babies, you must remember it.
That woman, your teacher, grilled you for 35 minutes,
question after question after question. She did it

in plain sight, in front of all the nurses, the residents,
the interns, the clerks, the other students. She wanted
you to answer incorrectly, wanted to shame you.

Question after question after question, you hid
behind correct facts and information. And when
she tired of the game, of trying to trip you up,

she announced to everyone that you were the best
minority student she had ever had. And you took it.
You wanted to be like a duck, to let it all wash off of you.

But even in that praise, there was venom. Even in praise,
she found a way to shame you, single you out. And you hid
behind correct answers. But now, you must make it personal.

# Self Portrait at 4 AM

And what help is the mirror? The mirror
is of no help at all, and neither is the water
I splashed into my eyes trying to silence

the sting and redness there. Help, I have
lost myself again. Night, morning, whatever.
I have seen this time so many times:

the wards quiet now except for the monitors
and their slow, steady beeping that matches
the bodies at rest. Sleep. I have been trying

to do just that. But in the call room mirror,
I cannot find myself. Those are not my eyes,
and the face is so clinical, the jaw suddenly

that of a prison guard, the mouth ready to
sound out the very word *clinic*. Who is
this man staring at me, the skin green

under the fluorescent lights, the bitter almonds
of his eyes now replaced by fear? Who was it
who wrote the best place to sight fear is the eyes?

Who knows. I can't remember anything
other than the fact I have to check on 231's
mental status every 45 minutes. The mirror

is of no use. It lies, dirty and spattered
with toothpaste and beard stubble and crud.
It lies. That man staring at me is not my friend.

That man wants to hurt me. He has
hurt me before. I have hurt myself.
God damn it, why is there is no soap in the dish?

# Sepsis

The fog has yet to lift, God, and still the bustle
of buses and garbage trucks. God, I have coveted
sleep. I have wished to find an empty bed

in the hospital while on call. I have placed
my bodily needs first, left nurses to do
what I should have done. And so, the antibiotics

sat on the counter. They sat on the counter
under incandescent lights. No needle was placed
in the woman's arm. No IV was started. It sat there

on the counter waiting. I have coveted sleep, God,
and the toxins I studied in Bacteriology took hold
of Your servant. When the blood flowered

beneath her skin, I shocked her, placed the paddles
on her chest, her dying body convulsing each time.
The antibiotics sat on the counter, and shame

colored my face, the blood pooling in my cheeks
like heat. And outside, the stars continued falling
into place. And the owl kept talking without listening.

And the wind kept sweeping the streets clean.
And the heart in my chest stayed silent.
How could I have known that I would never forget,

that early some mornings, in the waking time,
the fog still filling the avenues, that the image
of her body clothed in sweat would find me?

I have disobeyed my Oath. I have caused harm.
I have failed the preacher from the Baptist Church.
Dear God, how does a sinner outlast the sin?

# Documenting the Light

## I  RESPECT

I would rather fixate on the light in this room,
the way it shadows the edge of the bed
by the window, the way it gauzes everything
close to the window, the light refracting
through dirty glass.
                    But I am not here
to document the light for a painter in training.
The woman lying in the bed is dying.
There is nothing more I can do to prevent that,
the cancer in her ovaries now filling
her abdomen, and its virulent cells now
lodged in her liver, her bones, sheltering in
the basin of her skull against her brain.

You expect me to describe her, but I will not.
Instead, there are the walls outside Port Royal,
left long ago by Spanish settlers most
would refer to as pirates. The bricks in those walls
are crude, crumbling in the late afternoon
faster than expected. And against those walls,
the creeping flowers of the bougainvillea, its petals
rippling, from this distance, in a salty ocean breeze.
I am more than this vessel, and so is she.

And then there is Geneva, the Alps' white caps
bespeaking more than snow and the sight
of snow. There is the lake, almost frozen,
and the tree limbs bending under the weight of ice.
There is the ravine, half-filled with ice

and the memory of the body buried there.
No, I will not describe her or the way
in which she holds the blank notebook to her chest,
the way she refuses to look me in the face
this morning.
            We have looked on each other before
and seen things beyond our vision: she, a lady

in waiting, her servants yet to bring her tea;
me, the usher, the one who precedes the Angel
of Death. And if I say anything, it is
out of respect, always out of respect.
And if I touch her, it is to remind her of touch.
See her reddish-brown hair clinging to her face,
the sweat on her brow . . .
            No, I would rather
fixate on the light in this room, the way it shadows
the edge of the bed. And outside, the redwoods climb
out of this light, climb into the atmosphere like fire.

## II  I WILL COME FOR YOU IN THE MORNING

Sunday morning, and again I watch
the soul slowly evaporating from a vessel,
this woman whose eyes are like the eyes

of so many I have seen before: the skin
cooler than normal, the pumpkin-smell
of ketones on her breath. I am no friend

to Death, but I have seen her so many times
wandering the halls of the hospital,
an Englishwoman dressed like a nurse.

She has only the weakest contempt for me,
knows I spend so much of my time trying
to thwart what she calls simply the inevitable.

When she speaks to me, she does so in Spanish,
Hindi, or Cantonese, taunting me with the tongues
I cannot use. And still, I understand her, as if

the blood I cannot deny has a life of its own,
understands the words that spring from it
as it courses through my arteries and veins.

*Vendré para usted por la mañana como la luz*
*comienza a entrar su cuarto. Vendré calladamente.*
*Usted ni sabe que estoy allí.* And she is gone.

How many times now have I told you this?
What I cannot explain is the way in which
she never surprises me, the way in which

she makes her statements and then simply leaves.
Outside, fall has stolen the summer fog,
and the light is like gauze on the Headlands, the light

softening everything. In English, her words never seem
as menacing. You can never remember her words,
no matter how many times I've told you:

*I will come for you in the morning as the light*
*begins to enter your room. I will come quietly.*
*You will not even know I am there.*

# Against Divination

The smudge pots' smoke foretold more than the frost
we expected. Somewhere, in the center of the grove,
the men huddled together to examine the beautiful

yellow-green rot consuming the wayward branch
of the orange tree lying on the ground, examined
the break in the wood to divine something about

the nature of the situation. What surprises is their need
to know and predict peril. The drama of peril.
The pulse quickening, the blood pressure rising

until we feel the vibration in our knees. Divination:
by smoke, by fire, by mirror, by water itself. I have
forgotten which one truly predicts the certainty of peril.

And because you have opened up another, because you have
examined the cells of another, seen for yourself that we are
primarily water, do you, too, have that ancient power?

Today, the tears from the woman who tells me her doctor
gave her *six months*. Oh the gift of scrying, the gift of prophecy.
There are twelve types of rot for the orange tree,

but for the sake of mystery, I do not name them.
And for the way demise inches down the leaves
of the tiger lily, there are two names, verbs even.

That water holds the past, present, and future
is nothing new. Hippocrates, having examined tears,
suspected as much. Over the years, I have perfected

my suturing, have studied the tension of suture between
my hand and the resisting tissue, learned how it reveals
whether the closure will hold. The smudge pots' smoke

foretold more than we could ever have expected—
there would be frost and the threat of frost, fire
and the fire of rot racing throughout the grove.

My attempts to depict that scene were failures. Once,
I even tried to paint three doctors: one with his ears
sewn shut, another, his eyes. Likewise, I never finished

that painting, never completed the final doctor whose eyes
are dark, menacing, and wide. Someday, I will close his mouth
with red suture; I will conjure silence for that terrible oracle.

# Deus ex machina

Even the intangible can be broken.
Maybe it would be better for me to say
that things just go wrong, or that things

aren't always harmonious. At the start
of Saint-Saëns' *Danse Macabre*, a tritone,
an augmented Fourth, stands in for the Devil.

The violin itself must be tuned especially for this.
You think I am lying, but I am not lying.
Not the Ghost in the machine, but the Devil

in the instrument. Things go wrong. Things
sometimes go terribly wrong. And some of us
are attracted to this. We want to fix things.

As children, we were the ones who fixed anything—
mechanical, electronic, any malfunctioning machine
could be fixed, our tool-like fingers responding

to a fidgety, overactive imagination. Is that not
what calls some of us to the "healing arts,"
that strange desire to fix the human machine?

But all things broken cannot be fixed; the man,
whose eyes never meet my own, tells me
his spirit is broken, his spirit is crushed

(his words, not mine). And what can I
say to that?  What tools do I have to fix that?
Not these hands, not this brain

looking for other instruments besides these hands,
not this voice that is trying now to reassure him:
It will be okay . . . Believe me, things will be fine . . .

Nothing is working. He tells me this. Nothing
is working. And tomorrow, the nurse will offer me
a scrap of newspaper, will silently enter my office

and say nothing. When I read about how
he hanged himself in his garage, no amount
of tears or wringing of hands will fix it.

# Torn

There was the knife and the broken syringe
then the needle in my hand, the Tru-Cut
followed by the night-blue suture.

The wall behind registration listed a man
with his face open. Through the glass doors,
I saw the sky going blue to black as it had

24 hours earlier when I last stood there gazing off
into space, into the nothingness of that town.
Bat to the head. Knife to the face. They tore

down the boy in an alleyway, the broken syringe
skittering across the sidewalk. No concussion.
But the face torn open, the blood congealed

and crusted along his cheek. *Stitch up the faggot
in Bed 6* is all the ER doctor had said.
Queasy from the lack of sleep, I steadied

my hands as best as I could after cleaning up
the dried blood. There was the needle
and the night-blue suture trailing behind it.

There was the flesh torn and the skin open.
I sat there and threw stitch after stitch
trying to put him back together again.

When the tears ran down his face,
I prayed it was a result of my work
and not the work of the men in the alley.

Even though I knew there were others to be seen,
I sat there and slowly threw each stitch.
There were always others to be seen. There was

always the bat and the knife. I said nothing,
and the tears kept welling in his eyes.
And even though I was told to be "quick and dirty,"

told to spend less than 20 minutes, I sat there
for over an hour closing the wound so that each edge
met its opposing match. I wanted him

to be beautiful again. *Stitch up the faggot in Bed 6.*
Each suture thrown reminded me I would never be safe
in that town. There would always be the bat

and the knife, always a fool willing to tear me open
to see the dirty faggot inside. And when they
came in drunk or high with their own wounds,

when they bragged about their scuffles with the knife
and that other world of men, I sat there and sutured.
I sat there like an old woman and sewed them up.

Stitch after stitch, the slender exactness of my fingers
attempted perfection. I sat there and sewed them up.

# Notes

Epigraph: from the Second Movement of *The German Requiem* by
Johannes Brahms. "For all flesh is as grass..." 1 Peter 1:24.

"Windows": The Chagall Windows at the Art Institute of Chicago.
For Jacob Bertrand and Brett Gadsden.

"Blood": for Natasha Trethewey.

"The Bridge": for Jacob Bertrand.

"Nature": The thenar eminence is the mound below the thumb on the
palm, an eminence that corresponds to the muscles there that allow
for the multidimensional movements of the thumb.

"Paying Attention": for Jennifer Grotz.

"Quiet City": This poem is indebted to Aaron Copland's composition of the
same name.

"The Seventh Circle": The six words repeated at the ends of the lines in this
sestina come from Donald Justice's "On the Death of Friends in
Childhood."

"The Moss Garden": This poem is dedicated to both Megan Staffel and
Charles Baxter, whose lectures at the Warren Wilson MFA Program
for Writers in July 2006 provided me both the under-story and the
form for this poem.

"Wind": for all of my students.

"The Argument": This poem is dedicated to Ted Genoways.

"Few Shall Answer": Written in response to poems by Cate Marvin and
Rick Barot. The poem owes a quiet debt to Jorie Graham's
"San Sepulcro."

C. Dale Young practices medicine, serves as poetry editor of *New England Review*, and teaches in the Warren Wilson MFA Program for Writers. He is the author of *The Day Underneath the Day* (Northwestern, 2001) and *The Second Person* (Four Way Books, 2007), a finalist for the Northern California Book Award, the Lambda Literary Award in Poetry, and the *ForeWord Magazine* Book of the Year Award. He is a previous winner of the Grolier Prize, the Tennessee Williams Scholarship in Poetry from the Sewanee Writers' Conference, and fellowships from the Bread Loaf Writers' Conference, the Corporation of Yaddo, and the National Endowment for the Arts. His poems have appeared in many anthologies and magazines, including *Asian-American Poetry: The Next Generation, The Best American Poetry, Legitimate Dangers: American Poets of the New Century, American Poetry Review, The Atlantic Monthly, The Paris Review, Ploughshares,* and *POETRY.* He lives in San Francisco with his partner Jacob Bertrand.

"The Ether Dome": The Ether Dome is the site where medical students from Harvard University first learned surgical techniques at the Massachusetts General Hospital. It is supposedly where, on October 14, 1846, one of the first lessons in anesthetizing patients for surgery using ether was given. The first documented use of ether as an anesthetizing agent took place on March 30, 1842, under the direction of Dr. Crawford Long of Danielsville, Georgia. The term "anesthesia" was coined by poet-physician Oliver Wendell Holmes.

"Imprimatur": A pulmonologist is a physician trained in Internal Medicine who specializes in lung disorders. Many of them also work in critical care medicine and administer Intensive Care Units.

"The Personal": NICU is an acronym for Neonatal Intensive Care Unit.

"Sepsis": Sepsis is a life-threatening medical condition characterized by whole-body inflammation caused by infection. When the blood becomes colonized by bacteria, toxins may be released in massive quantities throughout the body that may cause death even if the bacteria themselves are eliminated by antibiotics.

"Torn": A Tru-Cut is a semicircular needle used to suture lacerations. They come in many sizes of bore to facilitate suturing of many different sizes of laceration.

# Acknowledgments

Grateful acknowledgment is made to the editors of the following publications, where these poems—sometimes in slightly different form—first appeared:

*Alaska Quarterly Review, American Poetry Review, Anti-, The Atlantic Monthly, Bat City Review, Bloom, Chelsea, Georgia Review, Gulf Coast, Harvard Review, Kenyon Review, Laurel Review, Linebreak, MiPOesias, New Hampshire Review, OCHO, Ploughshares, POETRY* ("*Corpus Medicum*"), *Poetry International, Slate, The Southern Review, Subtropics, TriQuarterly, Virginia Quarterly Review,* and *Yale Review.*

"Torn" appeared as the poem of the day for April 21, 2004, at the *Poetry Daily* web site.

"Torn" appeared as a limited-edition, fine letterpress broadside (Mad River Press, 2004).

"Torn" has been reprinted in the *Literature and Medicine* database maintained by New York University, Spring 2005 to the present.

"Stone and Fire" appeared as the web monthly poem for August 2005 at the *Verse Daily* web site.

"Torn" appeared in *Legitimate Dangers: American Poets of the New Century,* Michael Dumanis and Cate Marvin, eds. (Sarabande Books, 2006).

"Torn" has been reprinted in *Poetry Calendar 2007: 365 Classic and Contemporary Poems,* Shafiq Naz, ed. (Alhambra Publishing, 2006).

"*Recitativo*" was the Phi Beta Kappa poem for the 2007 Commencement Exercises at Ohio Wesleyan University.

"*Deus ex machina*" has been reprinted in *Poetry Calendar 2008: 365 Classic and Contemporary Poems,* Shafiq Naz, ed. (Alhambra Publishing, 2007).

"Sepsis" appeared in *The Best American Poetry 2008*, Charles Wright, ed., David Lehman, series ed. (Scribner, 2008).

"The Moss Garden" has been reprinted in *Poetry Calendar 2009: 365 Classic and Contemporary Poems*, Shafiq Naz, ed. (Alhambra Publishing, 2008).

"The Second Omen: Spring" appeared in *Best Gay Poetry 2008*, Lawrence Schimel, ed. (Lethe Press, 2008).

"In the Cutting Room," "Inheritance," "Or Something Like That," "*Recitativo*," "Sepsis," "The Bridge," and "Torn" were reprinted in the *Swallow Anthology of New American Poets*, David Yezzi, ed. (Swallow Press/Ohio University Press, 2009).

"In the Cutting Room" has been reprinted in *Poetry Calendar 2010: 365 Classic and Contemporary Poems*, Shafiq Naz, ed. (Alhambra Publishing, 2009).

As always, I would like to thank my beloved partner Jacob Bertrand, as well as my family and friends, for the support they have given me. For wonderful worl[k] environments that, in their ways, helped me create the space in which to writ[e] these poems, I would like to thank Lisa Boohar, M.D., my medical practice partner, the staff at the *New England Review*, and the rigorous writers who m[ade] up the Warren Wilson College MFA Program for Writers. I owe a significant debt to the Corporation of Yaddo for providing me the perfect setting and th[e] time that allowed me to assemble the first draft of this book. I also owe grat[itude] to the National Endowment for the Arts for a fellowship that allowed me th[e] chance to complete this book. I also must thank Jennifer Grotz for her care[ful] reading and suggestions that helped me put this book in its final shape. To the Bread Loaf Writers' Conference, I owe thanks for the 2009 Amanda Da[vis] Returning Fellowship. And finally, I am immensely grateful to my editor Martha Rhodes for her incredible support and belief in my work.

"The Ether Dome": The Ether Dome is the site where medical students from Harvard University first learned surgical techniques at the Massachusetts General Hospital. It is supposedly where, on October 14, 1846, one of the first lessons in anesthetizing patients for surgery using ether was given. The first documented use of ether as an anesthetizing agent took place on March 30, 1842, under the direction of Dr. Crawford Long of Danielsville, Georgia. The term "anesthesia" was coined by poet-physician Oliver Wendell Holmes.

"Imprimatur": A pulmonologist is a physician trained in Internal Medicine who specializes in lung disorders. Many of them also work in critical care medicine and administer Intensive Care Units.

"The Personal": NICU is an acronym for Neonatal Intensive Care Unit.

"Sepsis": Sepsis is a life-threatening medical condition characterized by whole-body inflammation caused by infection. When the blood becomes colonized by bacteria, toxins may be released in massive quantities throughout the body that may cause death even if the bacteria themselves are eliminated by antibiotics.

"Torn": A Tru-Cut is a semicircular needle used to suture lacerations. They come in many sizes of bore to facilitate suturing of many different sizes of laceration.

# Acknowledgments

Grateful acknowledgment is made to the editors of the following publications, where these poems—sometimes in slightly different form—first appeared:

*Alaska Quarterly Review, American Poetry Review, Anti-, The Atlantic Monthly, Bat City Review, Bloom, Chelsea, Georgia Review, Gulf Coast, Harvard Review, Kenyon Review, Laurel Review, Linebreak, MiPOesias, New Hampshire Review, OCHO, Ploughshares, POETRY* ("*Corpus Medicum*"), *Poetry International, Slate, The Southern Review, Subtropics, TriQuarterly, Virginia Quarterly Review,* and *Yale Review.*

"Torn" appeared as the poem of the day for April 21, 2004, at the *Poetry Daily* web site.

"Torn" appeared as a limited-edition, fine letterpress broadside (Mad River Press, 2004).

"Torn" has been reprinted in the *Literature and Medicine* database maintained by New York University, Spring 2005 to the present.

"Stone and Fire" appeared as the web monthly poem for August 2005 at the *Verse Daily* web site.

"Torn" appeared in *Legitimate Dangers: American Poets of the New Century,* Michael Dumanis and Cate Marvin, eds. (Sarabande Books, 2006).

"Torn" has been reprinted in *Poetry Calendar 2007: 365 Classic and Contemporary Poems,* Shafiq Naz, ed. (Alhambra Publishing, 2006).

"*Recitativo*" was the Phi Beta Kappa poem for the 2007 Commencement Exercises at Ohio Wesleyan University.

"*Deus ex machina*" has been reprinted in *Poetry Calendar 2008: 365 Classic and Contemporary Poems,* Shafiq Naz, ed. (Alhambra Publishing, 2007).

"Sepsis" appeared in *The Best American Poetry 2008*, Charles Wright, ed., David Lehman, series ed. (Scribner, 2008).

"The Moss Garden" has been reprinted in *Poetry Calendar 2009: 365 Classic and Contemporary Poems*, Shafiq Naz, ed. (Alhambra Publishing, 2008).

"The Second Omen: Spring" appeared in *Best Gay Poetry 2008*, Lawrence Schimel, ed. (Lethe Press, 2008).

"In the Cutting Room," "Inheritance," "Or Something Like That," *"Recitativo,"* "Sepsis," "The Bridge," and "Torn" were reprinted in the *Swallow Anthology of New American Poets*, David Yezzi, ed. (Swallow Press/Ohio University Press, 2009).

"In the Cutting Room" has been reprinted in *Poetry Calendar 2010: 365 Classic and Contemporary Poems*, Shafiq Naz, ed. (Alhambra Publishing, 2009).

As always, I would like to thank my beloved partner Jacob Bertrand, as well as my family and friends, for the support they have given me. For wonderful work environments that, in their ways, helped me create the space in which to write these poems, I would like to thank Lisa Boohar, M.D., my medical practice partner, the staff at the *New England Review*, and the rigorous writers who make up the Warren Wilson College MFA Program for Writers. I owe a significant debt to the Corporation of Yaddo for providing me the perfect setting and the time that allowed me to assemble the first draft of this book. I also owe gratitude to the National Endowment for the Arts for a fellowship that allowed me the chance to complete this book. I also must thank Jennifer Grotz for her careful reading and suggestions that helped me put this book in its final shape. To the Bread Loaf Writers' Conference, I owe thanks for the 2009 Amanda Davis Returning Fellowship. And finally, I am immensely grateful to my editor Martha Rhodes for her incredible support and belief in my work.

C. Dale Young practices medicine, serves as poetry editor of *New England Review*, and teaches in the Warren Wilson MFA Program for Writers. He is the author of *The Day Underneath the Day* (Northwestern, 2001) and *The Second Person* (Four Way Books, 2007), a finalist for the Northern California Book Award, the Lambda Literary Award in Poetry, and the *ForeWord Magazine* Book of the Year Award. He is a previous winner of the Grolier Prize, the Tennessee Williams Scholarship in Poetry from the Sewanee Writers' Conference, and fellowships from the Bread Loaf Writers' Conference, the Corporation of Yaddo, and the National Endowment for the Arts. His poems have appeared in many anthologies and magazines, including *Asian-American Poetry: The Next Generation*, *The Best American Poetry*, *Legitimate Dangers: American Poets of the New Century*, *American Poetry Review*, *The Atlantic Monthly*, *The Paris Review*, *Ploughshares*, and *POETRY*. He lives in San Francisco with his partner Jacob Bertrand.